Piano Play-Along

FAVORITE STANDARDS

ISBN 978-0-634-08391-4

HAL•LEONARD® CORPORATION
7777 W. BLUEMOUND RD. P.O. BOX 13819 MILWAUKEE, WI 53213

Visit Hal Leonard Online at
www.halleonard.com

CONTENTS

PAGE	TITLE	DEMO TRACK	PLAY-ALONG TRACK
4	Call Me	1	2
12	The Girl from Ipanema	3	4
9	Moon River	5	6
16	My Way	7	8
21	Satin Doll	9	10
24	Smoke Gets in Your Eyes	11	12
27	Strangers in the Night	13	14
30	The Way You Look Tonight	15	16

CALL ME

Words and Music by
TONY HATCH

If you're feel-ing sad and lone-ly, there's a serv-ice I ___

___ can ren-der. Tell the one who loves ___ you on-ly,

I can be so warm ___ and ten-der. Call me! ___

5

5

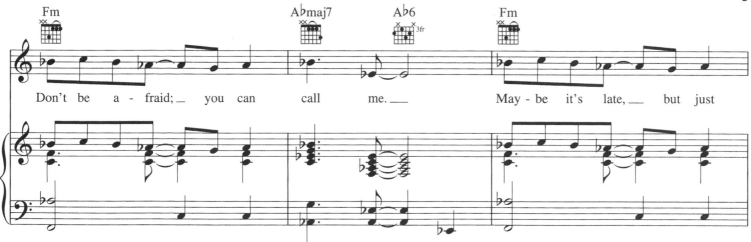

Don't be a - fraid;__ you can call me.__ May - be it's late,__ but just

call me.__ Tell me and I'll__ be a - round._____

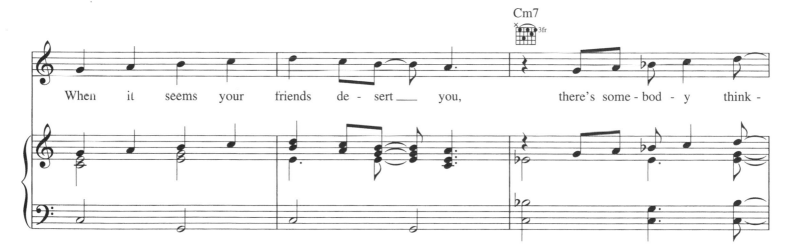

When it seems your friends de - sert__ you, there's some - bod - y think -

- ing of__ you. I'm the one who'll nev - er hurt__ you.

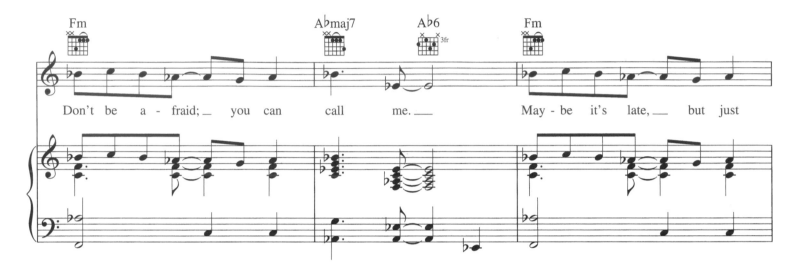

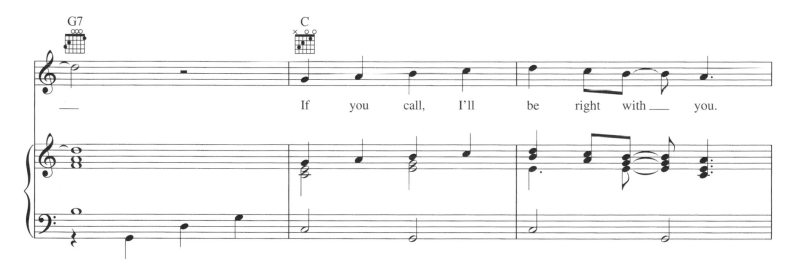

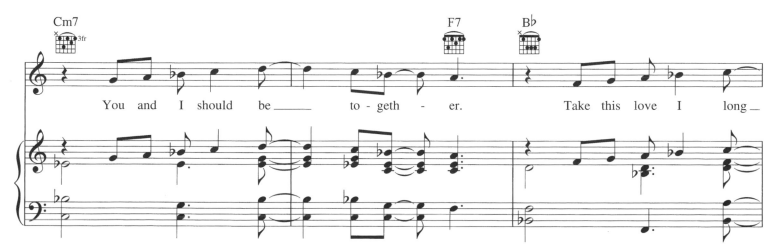

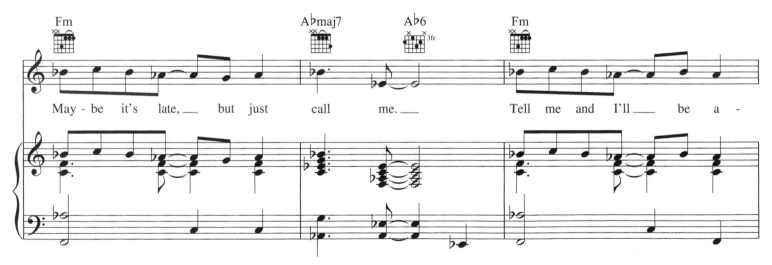

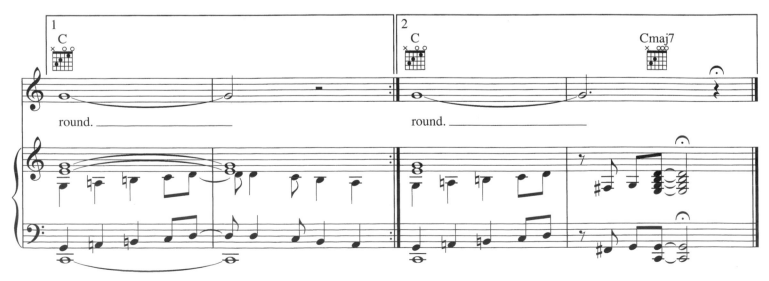

MOON RIVER

from the Paramount Picture BREAKFAST AT TIFFANY'S

Words by JOHNNY MERCER
Music by HENRY MANCINI

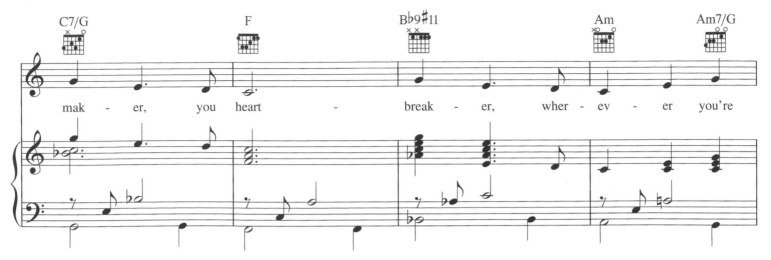

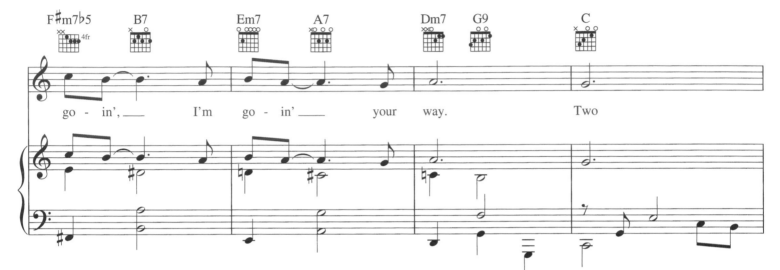

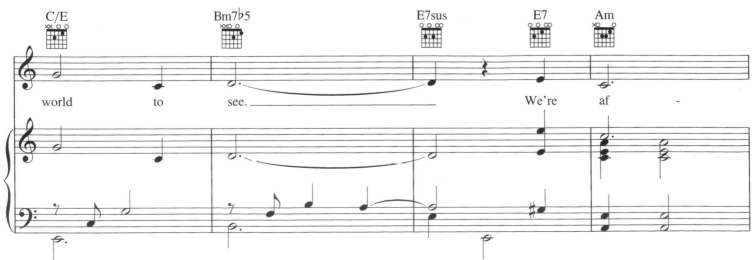

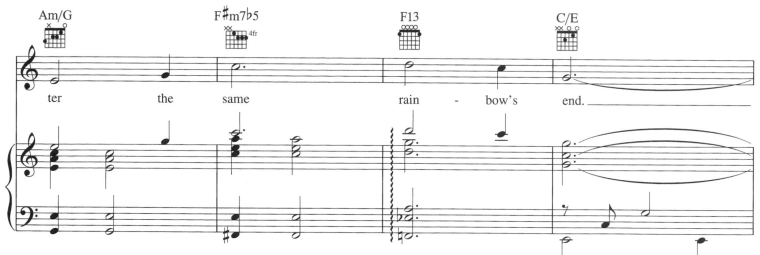

ter the same rain - bow's end.

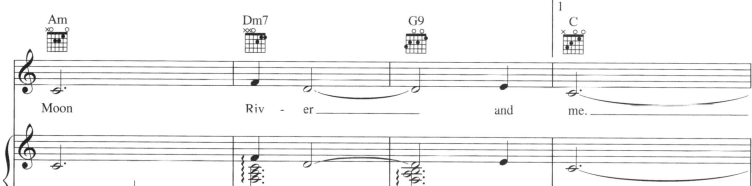

— wait - in' 'round the bend, _____ my Huck - le - ber - ry friend,

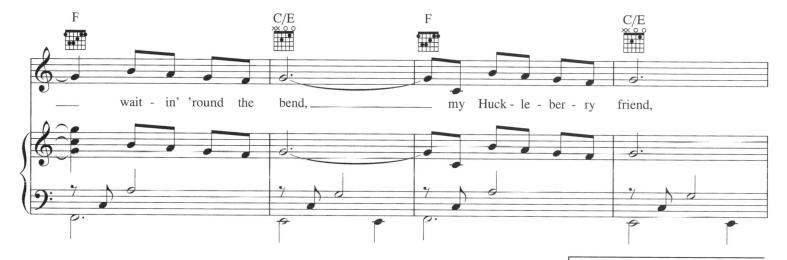

Moon Riv - er _____ and me. _____

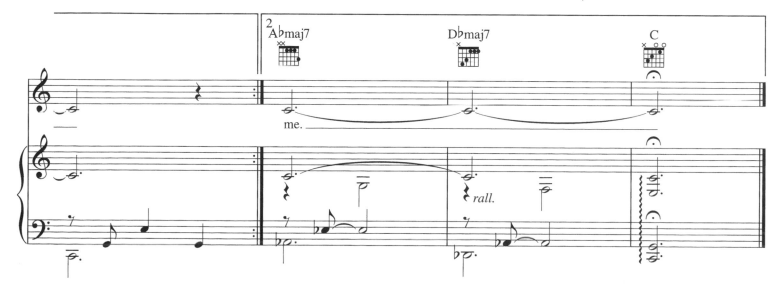

me.

THE GIRL FROM IPANEMA
(Garôta de Ipanema)

Music by ANTONIO CARLOS JOBIM
English Words by NORMAN GIMBEL
Original Words by VINICIUS DE MORAES

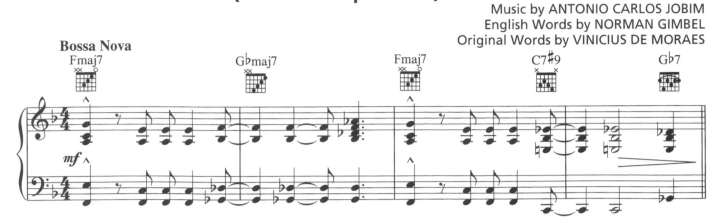

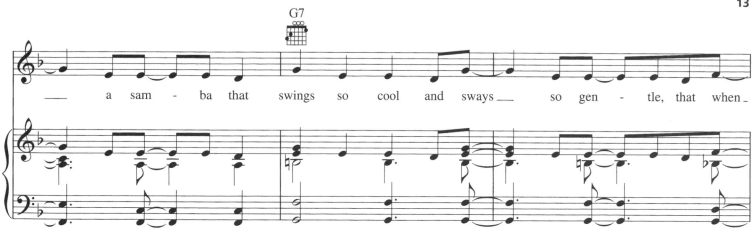

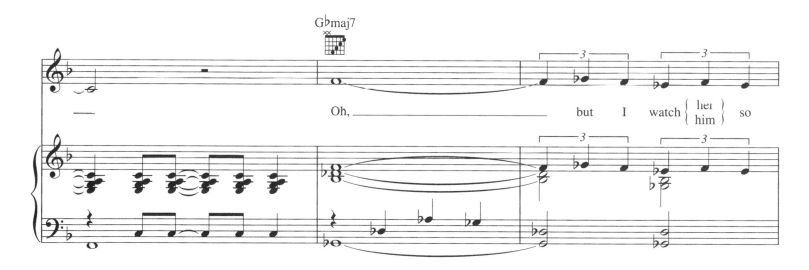

can I tell {her/him} I love {her?/him?} Yes, ___

___ I would give my heart glad - ly, ___

___ but each day when {she/he} walks to the sea, {she/he}

looks straight a - head not at me. Tall and tan and young ___

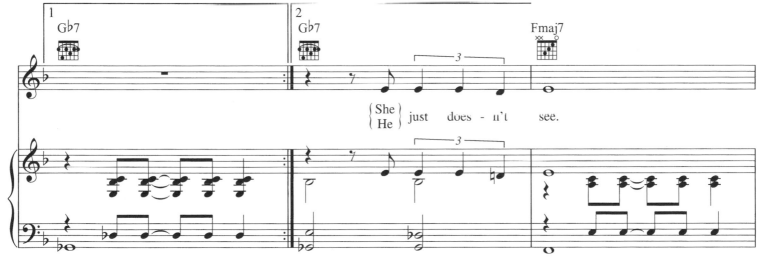

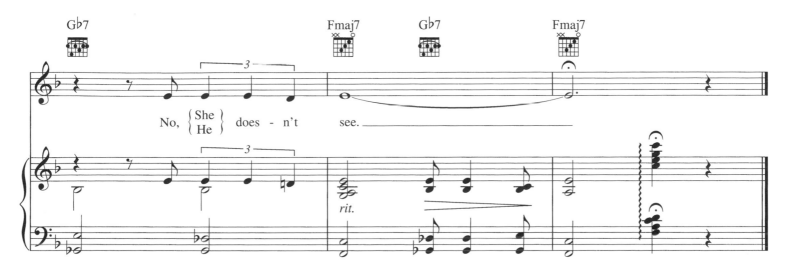

MY WAY

English Words by PAUL ANKA
Original French Words by GILLES THIBAULT
Music by JACQUES REVAUX
and CLAUDE FRANCOIS

18

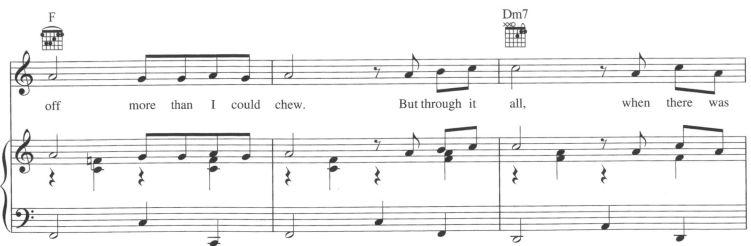

off more than I could chew. But through it all, when there was

doubt, I ate it up, and spit it out. I faced it

all, and I stood tall, and did it my

way. I've loved, I've laughed and cried, I've had my

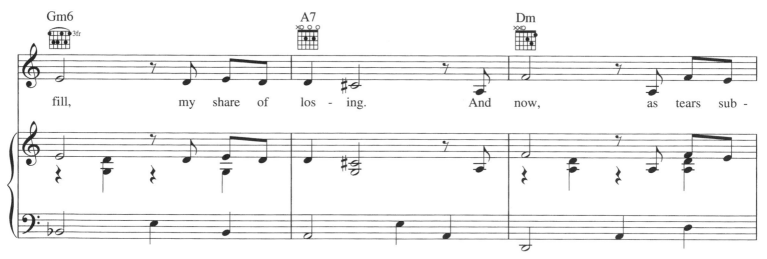

fill, my share of los - ing. And now, as tears sub -

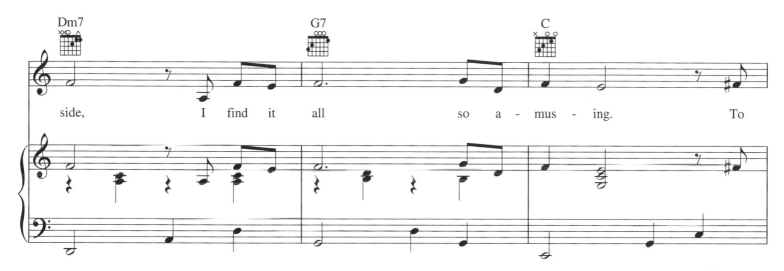

side, I find it all so a - mus - ing. To

think I did all that, and may I say, not in a

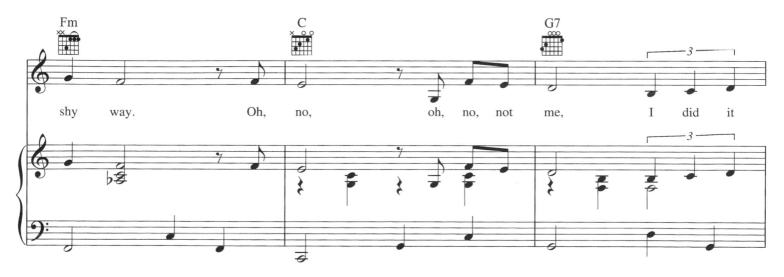

shy way. Oh, no, oh, no, not me, I did it

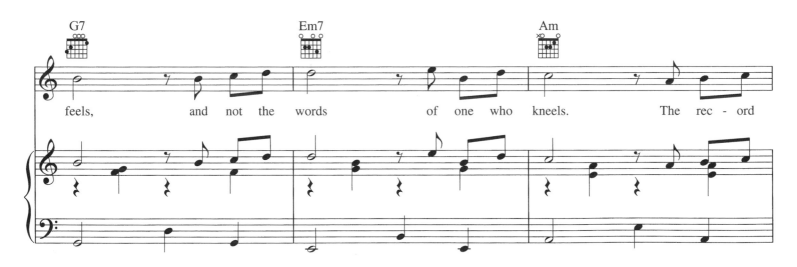

SATIN DOLL
from SOPHISTICATED LADIES

Words by JOHNNY MERCER and BILLY STRAYHORN
Music by DUKE ELLINGTON

Medium Swing

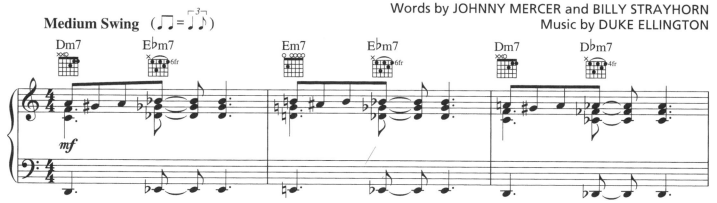

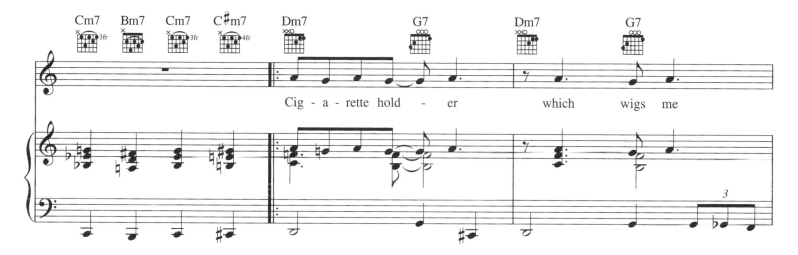

Cig - a - rette hold - er which wigs me

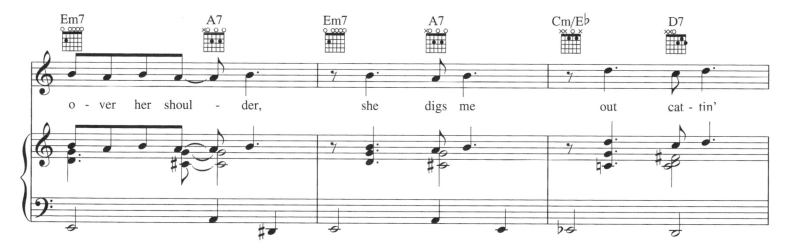

o - ver her shoul - der, she digs me out cat - tin'

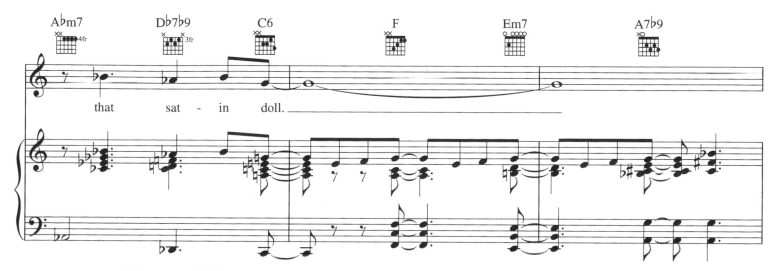

that sat - in doll.

Ba - by, shall we ___ go out skip - pin'? Care - ful, a - mi - go,

you're flip - pin'. Speaks Lat - in, that sat - in doll. ___

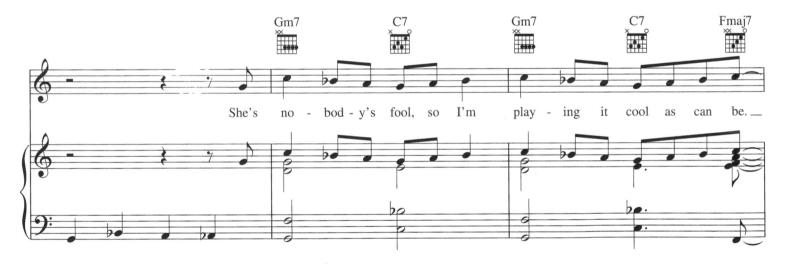

She's no - bod - y's fool, so I'm play - ing it cool as can be. ___

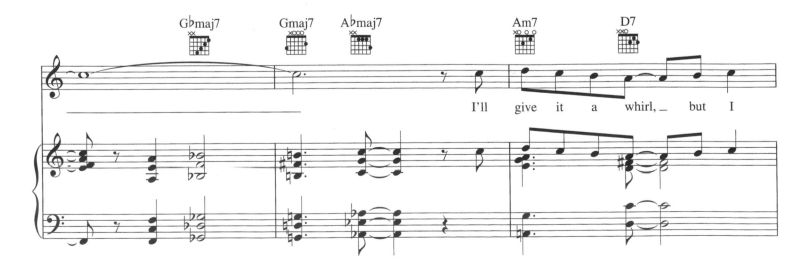

___ I'll give it a whirl, ___ but I

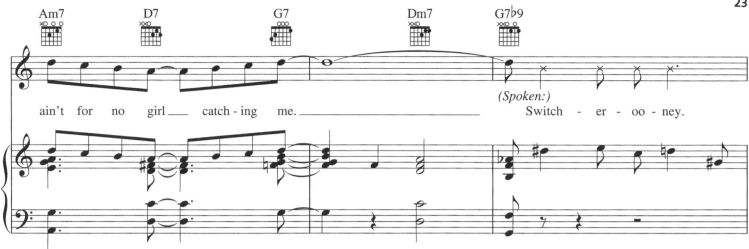

ain't for no girl ____ catch - ing me. _____ *(Spoken:)* Switch - er - oo - ney.

Tel - e - phone num - bers well you know, do - ing my rhum - bas

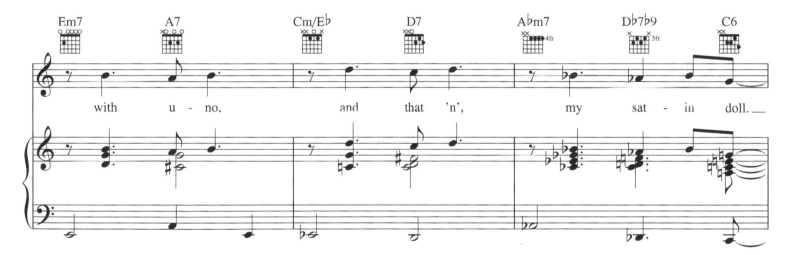

with u - no, and that 'n', my sat - in doll. ___

SMOKE GETS IN YOUR EYES

from ROBERTA

Words by OTTO HARBACH
Music by JEROME KERN

STRANGERS IN THE NIGHT

Words by CHARLES SINGLETON
and EDDIE SNYDER
Music by BERT KAEMPFERT

THE WAY YOU LOOK TONIGHT
from SWING TIME

Words by DOROTHY FIELDS
Music by JEROME KERN

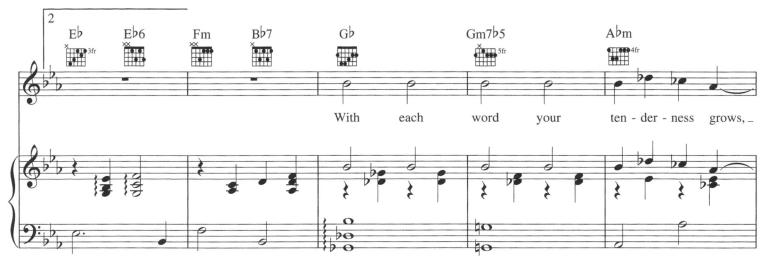

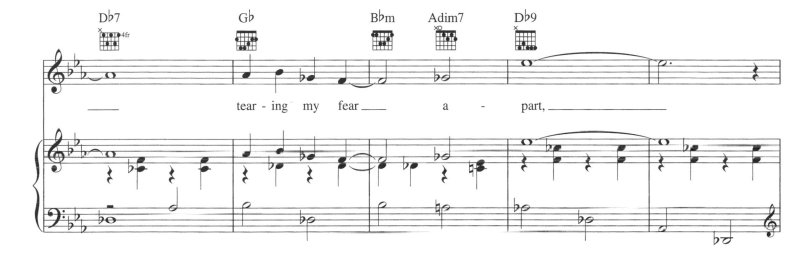

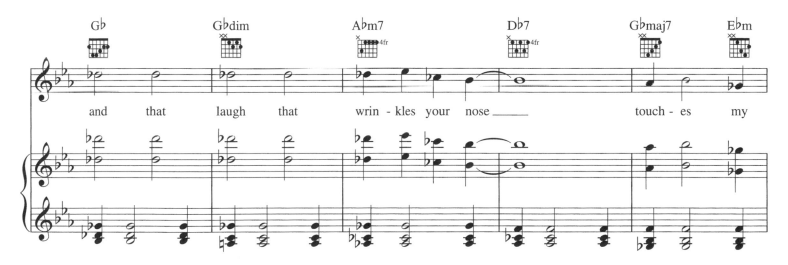

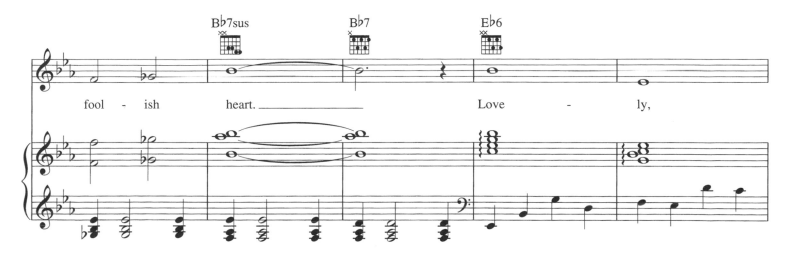

never, nev-er change, keep that breath-less charm,

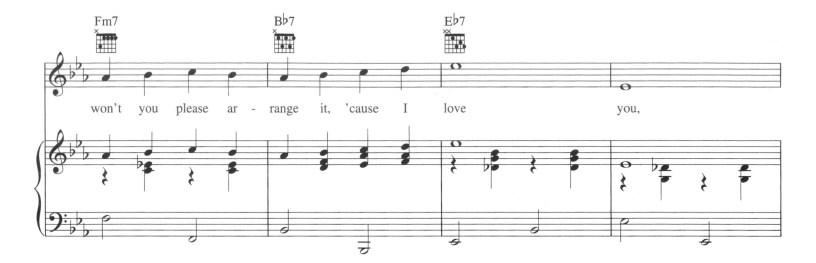

won't you please ar-range it, 'cause I love you,

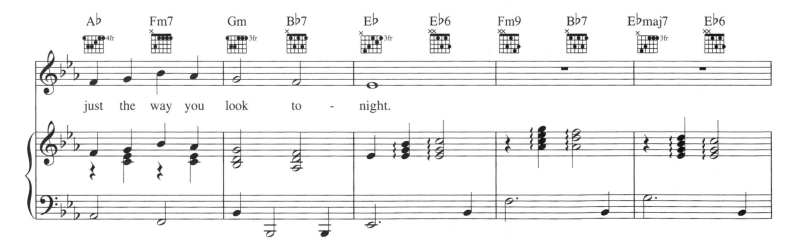

just the way you look to-night.

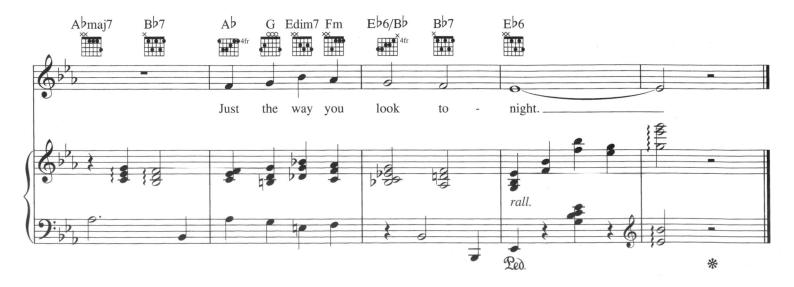

Just the way you look to-night.